THE WICHITA POEMS

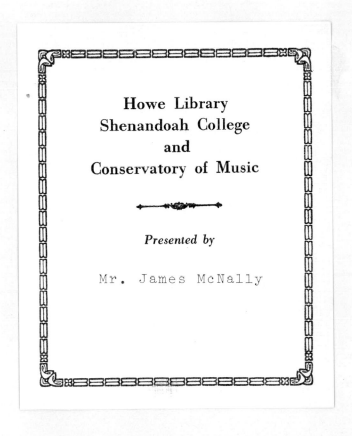

THE
WICHITA
POEMS

Michael Van Walleghen

UNIVERSITY OF ILLINOIS PRESS
Urbana   Chicago   London

LIBRARY OF CONGRESS CATALOGING IN PUBLICATION DATA

Van Walleghen, Michael, 1938–
    The Wichita poems.

    I. Title.
PS3572.A545W5   811'.5'4   75-19257
ISBN 0-252-00447-7
ISBN 0-252-00570-8 pbk.

"On Seeing the Abominable Snowman at the 1968 Kansas State Fair," *Northwest Review* XII, 1 (Fall–Winter 1971–72).

"The Possum," *Northwest Review* XII, 1 (Fall–Winter 1971–72).

"In the Elephant House," *The Southern Review* II, 1 n.s. (Winter 1966).

"The Tennis Match," *Poetry Northwest* IX, 1 (Spring 1968).

"Order," *North American Review* (March 1966).

"A Good Excuse," *The Southern Review* V, 4 (Autumn 1969).

"T.C.," (Wichita) *Mikrokosmos* no. 16 (1972).

"The Light," *The Southern Review* II, 1 n.s. (Winter 1966).

"Sometimes through the Frozen Trees," *The Southern Review* V, 4 (Autumn 1969).

"A Consequence of Earaches," *The Southern Review* (1975).

"The Traveler," *The Southern Review* V, 4 (Autumn 1969).

"Looking Back," *The Wichita Poems* (Iowa City: Stone Wall Press, 1973).

"The Moon Kites," *Poetry Northwest* IX, 1 (Spring 1968).

"In the Lion House," *The Wichita Poems* (Iowa City: Stone Wall Press, 1973).

"The Revolt of the Snowmen," *New Campus Writing*, ed. N. Miller (New York: McGraw-Hill, 1966). Used by permission of McGraw-Hill Book Company.

"Frankenstein's 4:00 a.m. Lament, or The Man Who Lives Downstairs," *The Southern Review* (1975).

"The Permanence of Witches," *The Southern Review* II, 1 n.s. (Winter 1966).

"The Man with Binoculars," *The Wichita Poems* (Iowa City: Stone Wall Press, 1973).

"That Summer We Were Last Together," *Northwest Review* XII, 1 (Fall–Winter 1971–72).

"Leaving," *The Wichita Poems* (Iowa City: Stone Wall Press, 1973).

"The Turning," *Steelhead* (Fall 1973).

"The Absence," *Northwest Review* (1975).

"Prairie Madness," *The Southern Review* V, 4 (Autumn 1969).

"Poem for My Great-Grandfather," *Heartland II* (De Kalb: Northern Illinois University Press, 1975).

"Where She Lives," *The Iowa Review* III, 2 (June 1972).

"The Sign on the Blackout Wall," *The Southern Review* (1975).

"The Prisoner," *The Southern Review* V, 4 (Autumn 1969).

"The Alligators," *The Iowa Review* I, 2 (June 1970).

For Joné

Contents

On Seeing the Abominable Snowman at the
   1968 Kansas State Fair 1
The Possum 2
In the Elephant House 4
The Tennis Match 6
Don Juan's 7
Order 8
A Good Excuse 9
T.C. 10
The Light 11
Sometimes through the Frozen Trees 12
A Consequence of Earaches 13
The Traveler 14
The Blue Quarry 15
Looking Back 16
The Moon Kites 17
In the Lion House 20
The Revolt of the Snowmen 21
Frankenstein's 4:00 a.m. Lament, or,
   The Man Who Lives Downstairs 23
The Permanence of Witches 25
The Dream She Tells This Morning 27
The Man with Binoculars 29
That Summer We Were Last Together 30
Leaving 31
The Turning 32
The Absence 33
Prairie Madness 34
Poem for My Great-Grandfather 36
Where She Lives 37
The Sign on the Blackout Wall 38

A Conversation 40
The Prisoner 41
The Alligators 43
The Confession 45

THE WICHITA POEMS

ON SEEING THE ABOMINABLE SNOWMAN
AT THE 1968 KANSAS STATE FAIR

They file by
whispering and pointing
but for the most part serious
like proper distant cousins
and he seems real enough
and after all, who knows?
Perhaps he's only sleeping there
in his coffin of cloudy ice.

In their neighborhoods of course
everything *is* serious, less
palpably surreal,
and death occurs to them
more often there; and really
what subtle permutations!
footsteps, past midnight
creaking in the snow
or in the window
something caught just vanishing
before their own reflections
focus in the glass. Or suppose
I drive at suppertime
through Hutchinson or Wichita
half blind, dazzled,
but going on forever
in that epileptic instant
when all the picture windows
glint inscrutably, golden,
as simply there
as tiny temple lakes
in the high Himalayas.

THE POSSUM

Suddenly
the dogs are listening.
It's after supper
and the trees too
stop for a moment
then dangerous, submarine
begin again — the last light
foreshadowing perhaps
the perilous arrivals
of the ship white moon.

Beneath the house
it's time. There, the truly
arboreal possum stirs
makes some shy commotion
through the leaves
or hesitates, lost . . .
although I feel him there,
huge in his apprehension,
and in his listening,
breathless as a neighborhood.

Block by block
in a moment, the streetlights
flicker on. A siren
somewhere wails. And sometimes
something pallid, slow,
a rat-like presence
shares these anxious changes
with me in the dark, —

or changes, stupidly forgets
the world is what it seems,
lets go and shuffles out
blinking like some last survivor
of the shipwrecked moon,
blind almost, helpless . . .
unless his eyes ignite
and finally focus
all the wild heartbeat's
faint fluorescence.

IN THE ELEPHANT HOUSE

In the elephant house
Heartbeats echo
And blackness moves
In the silent stalls.

These are the big dreams,
The whiskered mothers
Of the dark
No daylight eye accommodates.

These are the dancers
Of the easy death
Who rock like the wreckage
On some ocean floor.

Here the barracuda memories glide
Back and forth,
Back and forth,
In the unforgetting hulks

Of those disasters,
Overgrown with life,
That sway in the current
Of our own events.

How curious
Their tentacular trunks
Come snaking out.
How gently

We are hugged
To the twisted bars
And into that first sleep,
Where back and forth,

Back and forth,
Sick with the immensity
Of ourselves,
We dance.

THE TENNIS MATCH

Midnight. My serve.
A darkness stirs
in the far court —
the tricky competition
warming up, rehearsing now
with either hand
some deadly fore
or backhand shot.
The banked lights hum.
In the first rows
the faces tighten
and then diminish
into father's best
disapproving squint.
This helps. I wave
and give it all I've got.
The ball drones importantly
then leaps off . . . where?
Into nothing.
The void perhaps.
Perhaps never to return.
My father finishes his beer
bends the can
and leaves. The crowd leaves.
Doors slam. The last
beer cans tinkle softly
from the parking lot.
Tense, vibrant, competitive
I crouch and stare
into the far court
listening . . .
as the slow stars
revolve and flutter
over the blinding lights
which fix me here.

This last night
of the desert summer
drunk, fed up finally
with cowboy Jerry
and the marital histories
of the graveyard shift
at Magma Copper
I piss on the truck
and leave it there
stalled in moonlight
behind Don Juan's
two midnight miles
from anywhere
and closed. Later,
I'm stumbling in cactus
past the Apache Trailer Court
and down the dark gully
I've mistaken twice
for the shortcut home . . .
and then it's later
it's almost morning
or the ice blue
neon flicker
of the parking lot
behind Don Juan's
where I'm listening
finally, to something
eerily familiar: like birds
or someone whimpering
from one dark trailer
or another: *don't*
don't.

ORDER

for Catherine Davis

Surrounded
by the simple
undemanding order
of papered walls
of windmills waterwheels
trees descending
two by two
in the green weather
all that in me drifts
drifts steadily
towards the dark windows
where the afternoon
the aftermath of storm
and my own reflection float
indifferent and resigned
as the first star
the light that takes
blind light years coming
and sends us
lives and objects,
a vast destruction
toiling seaward
and past, their stiff
sharp blades unmoved,
the windmills
in the perfect weather.

A GOOD EXCUSE

It is snowing again.
A fine snow is sifting
Over the broken fields.

There is nothing more
That you can do.
You need not think

Again of moonlight
Or of the several voices
Which have called to you

Like voices from the moon.
Where would they have you go
That is not the same

Blank field? No, there is
Nothing left for you
But to stand here

Full of your own silence
Which is itself a whiteness
And all the light you need.

T.C.

May 1, 1946 –
December 25, 1971

T.C., believe me,
the night you died
I dreamt the Aurora
Borealis, and women
in agony, lost
on blinding ice.
But it was useless
and still half dark
and simply winter
there, in Wichita
when I looked out,
as if in nightmare,
on trees so still
so delicate in detail
your life occurred to me
like a stone kicked loose
into the tilted
attenuate reflections
of some black river
thick with leaves.

THE LIGHT

On a cloudy day
on a day the clouds
the lake the late
small sun seem stopped
and the gray birds
dive like stones
or drift high
petrified and small
against the light
against that symbol, metaphor
and old analogy
to which the heart
perpetually aspires,
on such a day,
even Icarus
might have turned
and walked into the marsh,
noticed by tall birds stalking
and the glittering fishes
that, cloud-like,
move away.

You look out
and sometimes
through the frozen trees
the moon is shining
or a light snow falls
or from the street
a conversation reaches you
or voices merely
none of which are separate
clear or quite resolved
yet nonetheless
so clearly understood
you turn and move away
reflecting smaller in the glass
a distance, an absence
a voice among the rest.

Insofar as earaches
are a consequence
of simply going out
hatless, before dawn
in the zero weather,
the car won't start,
and likewise, the day,
with news of war
in starving Bangladesh,
irrevocably proceeds. These
and other facts accumulate,
resembling, by afternoon
in the strange trees,
a flock of birds, starlings
which flutter down
by twos and threes
and graze the pale grass
like buffalo, one thinks —
forgetting, in an instant,
why it is we're here
or why we stay
staring finally out
at nightfall trees
the moon shines through
like a lightbulb
representing thought
in some cartoon.

Each town
its name dutifully pronounced
and the landmarks noted
at once dissembles as you leave
to become again the single town
you've never seen. And there
where the women stand
forever in their black dresses
their faces entirely lost
against the one white wall
that is the cracked memory
of a thousand faces
or a thousand walls,
the stiff birds slant
over La Via Dolorosa
and the closed cantina,
dust rises in the empty square,
and while you look
thinking how you might at least be spared
this public statue that resembles you,
it slowly changes back
to become once more the landscape
or the town in which you've just arrived,
places hopefully looked forward to
where nothing else is final
breaks the heart
or tells you you are no one here.

The phone rings
and from the bottomless
dead smooth water
of The Blue Quarry
he answers *help*
or *please* or *don't*
because god damn it
he's really drowning now
and it's no joke
it's really curtains
shoes the clock
beside the radio
it's his whole room
in fact, convincing
as a baby's towel
his little boat perhaps
and all that water
where marble cliffs
and cliff close trees
repeat themselves
like so much scenery
on a dinner plate.

LOOKING BACK

Looking back, it seems to you
it was always winter
where you stood . . . but really,
was it only you
the streetcars sang to
passing blocks away? The houses
seemed always inessential then
like houses in a play . . . but really,
was it only you
who stood there, listening . . .
some great elephant seal
they'd caught, stuffed
and put out on display?
Looking back, over the houses
and through that silence
suffered as a child,
his eyes, into yours
stared utterly confused —
as if, just now,
beyond the terribly familiar
weather of that world,
he'd somehow guessed
your presence here.

O solitude whence come the stones
of which, in the Apocalypse, the city
of the great king is built.

Are you conscious . . . of the stages
of your growth? Can you fix the
time when you became a babe, a boy,
a youth, an adult, an old man?
Every day we are changing, every
day we are dying . . .
—St. Jerome

This is Maple Grove
and no one comes here much —
a few kids now and then
or from the new
neighboring apartments
some retired fireman perhaps
to exercise his dogs.
No one seems to mind.
They bury now across the road.

Well, this spring, after months
of pacing in your room
or staring absently
at books at letters saved
or never sent
or looking simply
at whatever monuments
of absence distance or decay
the day might balance nicely
on the back of a hand,
you've come once more
to Maple Grove, reading out

17

as absently the names
you'd memorized last fall
and are vaguely pleased
that things look much the same
that the same few graves,
the smaller headstones
near the fence, remain
decked sadly out
in last year's green
and plastic evergreens
and that the mausoleums
still manage somehow to suggest
a small grimy compromise
between an old unhappy school
and its adjacent church.

Somewhere beyond the mausoleums,
fluttering somewhere
over the used up place
where the monuments
have settled, tilting
oddly in the weeds,
two kites are rising
are floating like the moons
you might imagine
keep rising still
over childhood's leveled
and disremembered town
the silly moons of love
moons of that moonlit
and leafy entropy
of random stones
towards which the blank
white and real moon

or even love itself
so irretrievably depend.
Still, how colorfully they speak
our need for flags
bright signs and metaphor —
for such simple
celebrations of the weather
as the forever hovering
and impossible angel
might afford those saints
like bald Jerome
who, though sick
and altogether weary,
nonetheless sat quiet
in his wilderness,
neither wary of the lion
nor bruised enough
with the wisdom of stones.

A part of you grows up
and stands apart
and grows less mindful
of the child . . . unless
to notice sometimes,
in zoos or in museums,
how you are drawn
irresistibly past
all the pits barriers
and cages of the harmless
to whatever is gigantic
or indisputably sovereign.
And what great need is born
or answered in you then?
In the lion house
at feeding time
when the lioness roars out
against the loud close limits
imposed upon her grace
suppleness and power,
what part of you,
glancing quickly at the rest,
turns then with careful interest
toward the keeper
the man with the panther tattoo?

It shall be at suppertime
a time of silence
of long shadows.

The children shall discover them
moving imperceptibly
towards the house,

their dark eyes wide
with the rage
of passionate men

who have lived too long
in the necessary weather.
And a slight agitation

of their arms
shall pronounce them
anxious to embrace

some warmer life —
the women they know
survive

in the houses
paralyzed
in some antarctic

of cold habit
where the impotent shapes of love
are slept with

like real men —
and they shall sway forward
huge

from the assembled dark
and the children shall hear them,
the small sound

of furious feet
in the periodic wind,
and it shall not be easy

when they arrive
to look like fathers
like fathers

who have come home
   to eat
   to tease the children
   to go to bed with wives

who have stared all winter
into the yard
and waited.

FRANKENSTEIN'S 4:00 A.M. LAMENT, OR, THE MAN WHO LIVES DOWNSTAIRS

Yes, of course
I am a wretch,
stitched together
as I am, ill-made,
criss-crossed, a head
on someone's body, ears
on someone's head, a hand
that flutters up
from nowhere
like a dark wing
and murders the innocent
as they sleep, sleep
in their beds. No doubt
you've even seen me,
staring maniacally back
from rain-dark windows
or the bathroom mirror,
a face like death
warmed over, breathing,
the perfect likeness
of everything despised . . .
you know precisely
who I am. But listen,
can you hear me,
you, up there? I need
no less than you
forgiveness, love,
a place to stand —
yet even in this
my heart beats
like the clattering echo
of some kicked

23

and spinning chair
and already now
whatever it was
I was meant to say
becomes instead
a methodical shattering
of dishes, ashtrays, lamps,
a ripped out telephone,
becomes as wrong
as someone screaming,
you, phoning the police,
and the littlest children
hiding in the hallway closet.

The moon
stars and weather
happen as they always have,
and between old Salem
where the pale women
burned like leaves
and this midwestern town,
the ash of dark reality
has sifted, settled down
and become the neighborhood
at suppertime,
the wives we take to bed.
And I think
those trivial lives
that gathered once
among the ferns,
among the oaks
that scattered near the sea
at Salem
were not more evil than our own,
but neither could the men
have better understood
what drives a woman
not to love.
Tonight, in black,
on a broomstick riding,
the witch the watcher
the spiteful other
coasts out and out
along the frigid edges of her life,
and these abandoned shapes,
these faithful wives we love
and learn to hate,

this girl that moans
beneath me, far away,
this body burned
and sick to death
of burning, turns
in the pale half-light,
in the fires
hissing near the sea
at Salem.

She tells me
it was evening
and she was out
by herself, walking
through a garden.

There were statues:

A centaur a bear
Beauty and the Beast
and at the far end
through the fuzzy
barely budding limbs
of the silver maples
she could see a house
of many windows.
It was her house
she says, and turns
and looks at me
so that I too
can see it clearly:
She is the moon's
lost princess
his only daughter
and we've just met
walking through the garden
on some meatpacking
dead millionaire's estate.

Next door, my neighbor
on her way to church
sings "Rock of Ages."
The Sunday paper
slams into the door,
and I remember beauty
like the bronze gorilla
who finally takes her
in his arms and whispers:
O hummingbird, chicken sparrow
indigo bunting, it's spring
I'm lonely, I love you.

As I remember it
both of us were nuts
and for years it seems
just weeks away
from your divorce.
Meanwhile (and God knows why)
we hid from everyone:
our friends the paperboy
my breathless neighbors
listening through the wall
or sometimes, rarely,
blessed by accident perhaps
with one full day
we'd drive out nervously
for picnics
to some landscape
from a book on Kansas
near a river
fifty million years ago.

Or so it seemed
in all that May
late morning light —
despite the evidence:
beercans footprints
and even someone's
tethered catfish once, —
someone with binoculars perhaps
who may have parked
just right
and barely glimpsed us
from the road.

After the insults
the arguments the hopeless
night-long talks
after I was sleeping on the couch
I rose for work each day
went out, and in a willed
and desperate kind of sleep,
stepped down from the bus at dawn,
turned left at the slaughterhouse
and walked up the street
of the abandoned buildings,
past the grocery store
the Acme Shoe Repair
and now and then a house,
its nineteenth-century
gables boarded up
and the long grass
swinging hushed and violent
in the cluttered yard.
But I remember most
how the distant cries
of pigs and cattle
seemed right
and almost human there
and always louder
as that summer's sun
broke over the last rooftops,
the whole lost neighborhood
we kept building till the end.

LEAVING

"In any case," he said,
"it was just personal."
—The Great Gatsby

How good it was
when I was leaving
to watch at first
the winglight blinking
and later too
when we'd finally turned
over the last
far outskirts of the city
and banked back west
how good it was
to have the moon right there
and sailing with me
near the cold North Star —
contingent as arrival
and painful too,
like your porchlight
shining through the park
those summer nights
when I still prayed
for your divorce
and you still promised —
ethereal as angels
on the pinpoint
of departure.

THE TURNING

When the river turns
and gathers darkly
at the bank
and the dry grass
bends exhausted
to the slow water's edge
and a few leaves float
farther out
at the end of autumn,
still the red
revolving focus
of all that water,
I dream perpetual ice
and the white beginning
when nothing moves,
when neither the river
nor the leaves
nor the trees
where the leaves might be
at the end of autumn
at the edge
of all that water
can make me think of you,
the slow turning
of the world we were.

THE ABSENCE

I'm saving letters
from a strange country
where it's always raining
where it never rains enough
where all my love is blond today
lonely, dressed up perhaps
in her yellow raincoat
and looking out for spring
in the cat-tailed ditches
where it makes no difference
where a lost glove is enough
where everything is lost
where the long days, fields
and hillsides blur
into a single desolation
and the sheep go on forever
just standing dumbly
in the rain — where letters
begin with yesterday
and the continuing
perversities of weather
the black still-born lamb
the dog who slaughters
and lately
the dream of broken toys.

For those who waited,
who lived here first
before the towns
when the few sod huts
scattered out
and scarcely rose
above a sea of grass,
it must have seemed
a great relief
for surely they might have guessed
when nothing more seemed odd
or quite familiar
how one dreadful night
at the white moon's rising
it must come upon them:
nor could they stop
that constant wind
from howling out of nowhere
and howling as it used to
before the old
terrible sea of leviathan
vanished into dreams
that just as surely woke
and left those women listening
beneath the wind
beneath the weather
to the hushed and violent
rushing of the grass.

In my mind I see them
alone and singing as they walk
until at last
those figures lose themselves
in all that moves to meet me here
where heat melts the highway
and the slow wheat nods
on either side for miles.

It snowed hard
that whole long winter.
At Eagle Harbor, Mohawk,
Calumet, the mines
and lumber camps
all closed. Mother
still remembers that,
and children starving,
diphtheria, lice. One night
her little sister died
and the next,
in that pitch black
beyond the last house
that ends her memory
of that town, the lake
that never freezes
froze. It looked,
I think, something
like the sky
above Detroit
on payday nights,
Fridays, when the moon,
occasional, looked always
like the moon
of absent fathers —
white, varicose,
bulging like a fetus,
or like the eye
of some lumberjack
cheapskate drunk
dying on the ice.

This is the time when the man
and the moment come together.
—Richard M. Nixon

When Mr. Nixon
comes to dinner
it's Wichita, someplace
lonely, some anxious kitchen
where it hums
like dwindled flies
warming on a window sill.
In the next apartment
the whole population
of some other planet
fuck, a commotion
cheerless as those cheers
heard distantly
on football afternoons —
or something stumbles
thoughtless, half Dracula
and half November,
through the bedroom mirror:
the pale husband
reciting in a voice
as clear as water
draining in a sink
of severed hands
why the lightbulb
in the lamp is loose
or on the table
why the bread just sits there
soft, inexplicably white
beside the broken radio.

THE SIGN ON THE BLACKOUT WALL

—Wichita, 1968

When I think these days
to write of it
I want always to begin:
O Wichita! O cold
disheveled city
of my sleep! But Chekhov
who truly understood
such things — Gromov
going mad for instance,
so simply, irrevocably
insane and beautiful —
what would he have said?

It's high noon
in Wichita, 1968,
the long summer
of my thirtieth year,
and time is running out.
For instance: the bartender's
languid pet piranha
bites his crippled lunch
in half and half
the students here
are probably police.
Still, I'm sitting
where I always sit,
the airplane roaring
somewhere overhead
is none of my affair,
and if anyone should ask,
I'll simply tell them no,
I can't read, and no,

I don't know the spastic,
Carlos, passed out
beneath the Russian sign
which translates: Stop!
Identify yourself!

A CONVERSATION

When she was afraid enough
to say anything, she said
it was all right, really,
and really, she thought,
as far as he was concerned,
the urinous boathouse
in the park with no moon
seemed just perfect —
but then he got quiet, he
kept fussing with his gloves
and she remembers now
that it seemed a long time
before the pattering of leaves
that filled the intervals
of their difficult breathing
finally, mercifully stopped.

After that, she remembers
waking up, screams, weeds
and the nightmare water
where the imagination shrinks
like a foot touching shit,
dead animals, slime,
all the sharp glass
in that lily-choked lake —
or it reaches blindly out
toward some shadow, some voice
it only half believes,
anything, her arm for instance,
the scar in two places
where she's fended off
the ax.

THE PRISONER

Above the elm trees
parking lots
and the tiny
overtended lawns
of city hall
the prisoner looks out
imagining as always
his dry usual life
igniting differently
into the old violence
his true substance
blazing beautifully for once
down the expensive
and darkening streets
of some new suburbia
some nicer Wichita
where at last
the hard-nippled housewife
rises from her bath
and knowing . . . yes . . .
motions him around the back.

It's noon. It's five o'clock.
It's night again
and the familiar moon
rising over the distant
routine noise of cars
and people passing
drifts whitely now
or reveals merely
through its feathery vapors

silky and black
the hard white curve
of its various parts.
And he's still there
resting, exhausted now
by the full weight
of that helpless other
by the slow violent dance
of some enormous life
he must watch forever.

And his fascination is our own
the pure inarticulate fascination
of the vaguely terrified
those of us who have kept on watching —
nonetheless and without pity
the heat-mad tar-foot sparrow
who hops himself to death
in the shopping center
parking lot.

THE ALLIGATORS

Feigning sleep,
to the casual eye
more dead than alive,
they wait. On them,
like a dinner plate
forever dropping,
all things depend.
One sees it clearly
in the eyes
of certain women.
After a time
not even their children
can pull them away.
I have seen them
standing tensely there
as at a window:
my mother
my grandmother looking out
one hand floating absently
among the dishes,
and the sink, the sink
soft-sucking things
it can't quite swallow.
I have seen them standing there
as rigidly as birds
who feel too late
the almost imperceptible
undulation of stagnant water.
When at last
they lift their heads

I've felt the whole zoo listen:
a neighborhood at dark
listening to streetcars
the far factories whistling
children, a lifetime
the perfectly indifferent
closing in.

THE CONFESSION

He reads anything,
pretends to work, think,
or falls asleep till noon,
still waiting for the mail . . .
which never comes to Wichita
in mid-July, where it stinks
of last night's supper
or something even worse,
something cats might leave
behind the stove. Anyway,
certainly today, he thinks,
he'd just get up, get dressed,
and write her one last letter
explaining everything. This time
he'd be better, he'd confess
how everything was all his fault:
the wind for instance, the heat,
the water tank that hovered
like a luminous evil cloud
above the front lawn trees
and trees that wouldn't stop
but kept repeating in the wind
that empty morning's dream
of antique windmills
that turned for nothing
in the brilliant air. Later,
he might confess his dream
of the laid-off uncles,
their missing fingers,
the hands that won't come clean,
confess their brutal, boring,
endless afternoons of euchre
on the porch. He'd confess

to anything almost. He'd say
how even she reminded him,
in her absence, of someone
lying naked, on a bed like his,
a snapshot he'd kept hidden
as an adolescent in a book
picturing archaic reptiles
of the great swamp — or someone
wearing panties, bending over,
smiling always past her knee
and out the little window
of a coal bin in Detroit . . .
where he couldn't move
where voices echoed vaguely
from the porch, where everything
was all his fault; and upstairs,
on the dining room Sunday table
the mother's day daisies
were dying in a white vase
and O, become a sad posy
of funereal flowers.

Poetry from Illinois

History Is Your Own Heartbeat
Michael S. Harper (1971)

The Foreclosure
Richard Emil Braun (1972)

The Scrawny Sonnets and Other Narratives
Robert Bagg (1973)

The Creation Frame
Phyllis Thompson (1973)

To All Appearances: Poems New and Selected
Josephine Miles (1974)

Nightmare Begins Responsibility
Michael S. Harper (1975)

The Black Hawk Songs
Michael Borich (1975)

The Wichita Poems
Michael Van Walleghen (1975)

제